BE POSITIVE good things are GOING TO HAPPEN

igloobooks

Published in 2020
First published in the UK by Igloo Books Ltd
An imprint of Igloo Books Ltd
Cottage Farm, NN6 0BJ, UK
Owned by Bonnier Books
Sveavägen 56, Stockholm, Sweden
www.igloobooks.com

0920 001
2 4 6 8 10 9 7 5 3 1
ISBN 978-1-80022-570-1

Designed by Simon Parker
Edited by Natalie Graham

Printed and manufactured in China

NOTHING IS IMPOSSIBLE. ONLY IMPROBABLE.

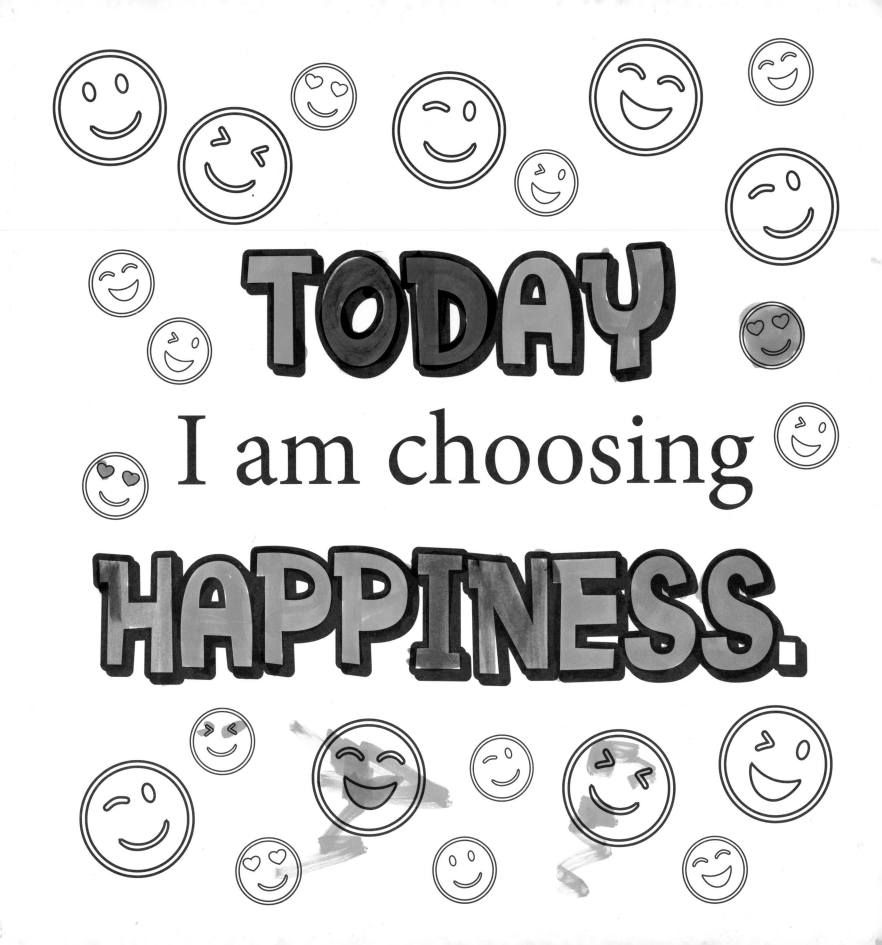

DIFFICULT ROADS LEAD TO
BEAUTIFUL DESTINATIONS.

The best view comes after the hardest climb.

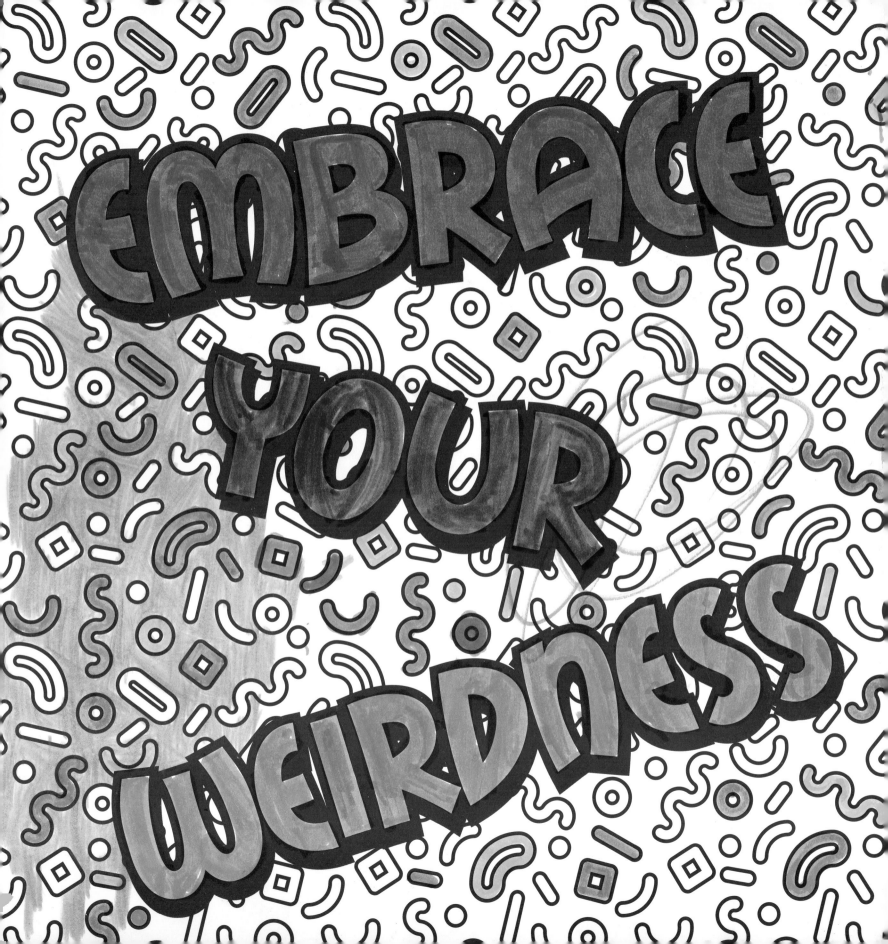

We age not by years, but by stories.

Always start your day with a cup of positivitea

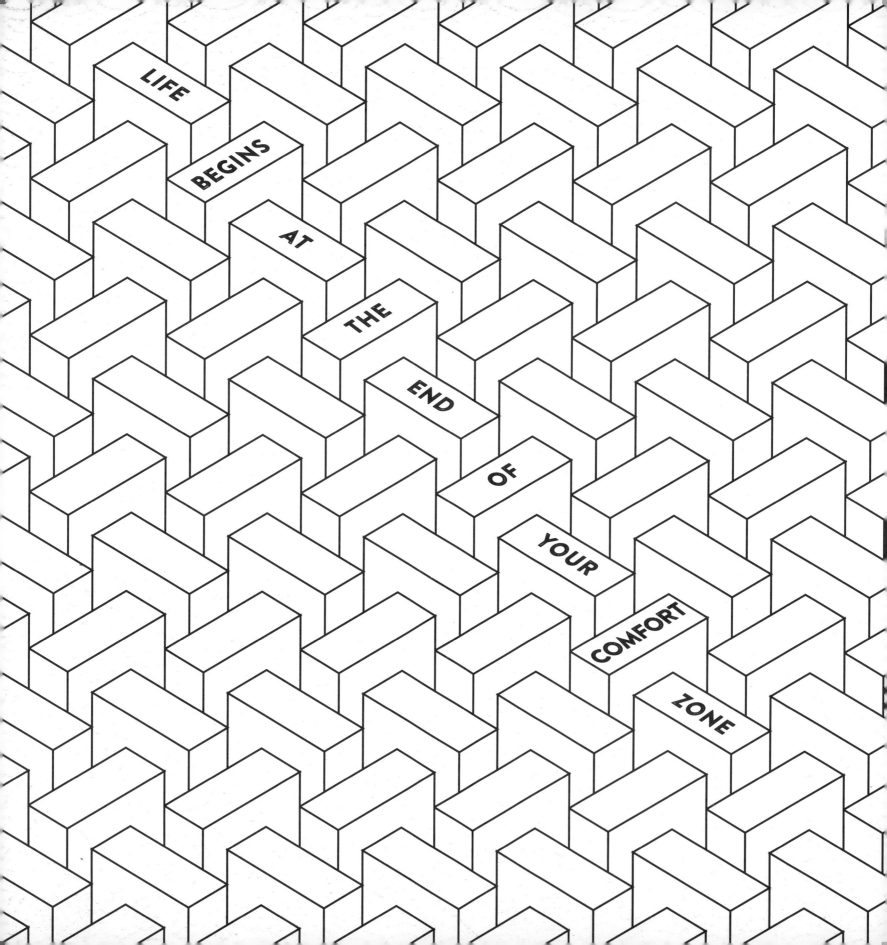

LIFE BEGINS AT THE END OF YOUR COMFORT ZONE

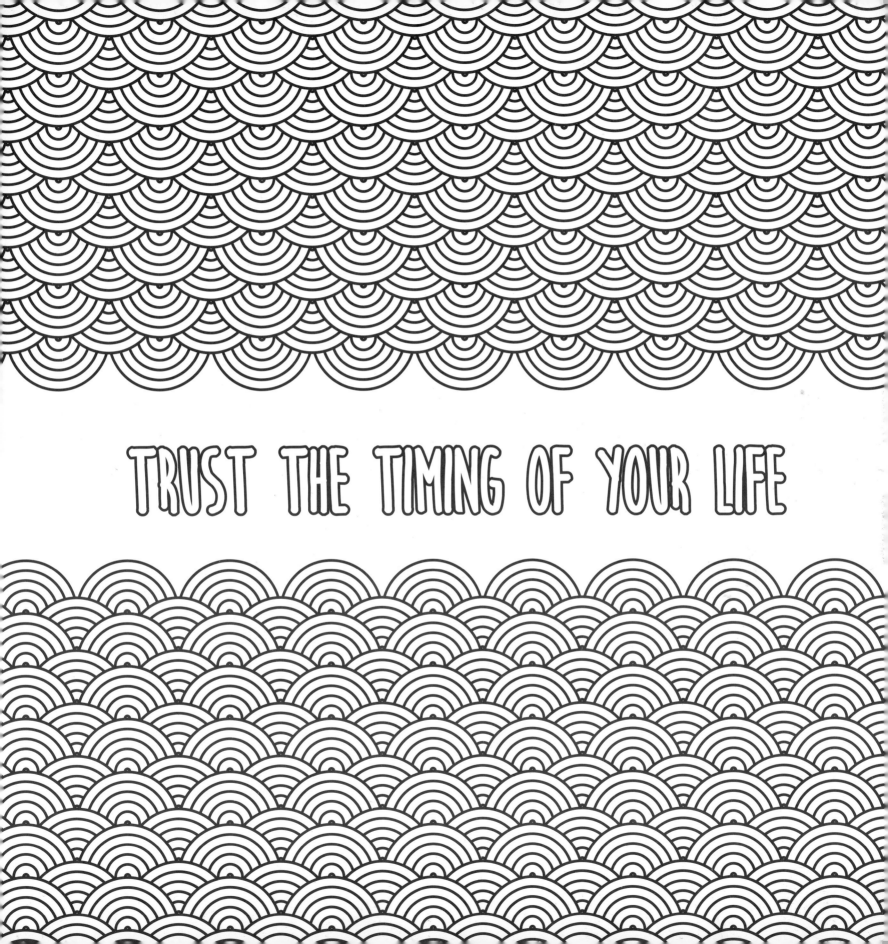

TRUST THE TIMING OF YOUR LIFE

Find the beauty in all that is around.